GOD MADE MAN

SCOTT SILVERII, PHD

© 2020 Scott Silverii

All rights reserved. No part of this publication may be reproduced, distributed, or transmitted in any form or by any means, including photocopying, recording, or other electronic or mechanical methods, without the prior written permission of the publisher, except in the case of brief quotations embodied in critical reviews and certain other noncommercial uses permitted by copyright law. For permission requests, contact Five Stones Press or Dr. Scott Silverii

All Scripture quotations, unless otherwise indicated, are taken from the New American Standard Bible, ©1960, 1962, 1963, 1968, 1971, 1972, 1973, 1975, 1977, 1995 by The Lockman Foundation. Used by permission.

Other versions used are:

KJV—King James Version. Authorized King James Version.

NIV—Scripture taken from the Holy Bible, New International Version®. Copyright © 1973, 1978, 1984 by International Bible Society. Used by permission of Zondervan Publishing House. All rights reserved.

First Edition

Publisher: Five Stones Press, Dallas, Texas

For quantity sales, textbooks, and orders by trade bookstores or wholesalers contact Five Stones Press at publish@fivestonespress.net

Five Stones Press is owned and operated by Five Stones Church, a nonprofit 501c3 religious organization. Press name and logo are trademarked. Contact publisher for use.

Dr. Scott Silverii's website is scottsilverii.com

Printed in the United States of America

DEDICATION

To the first, ultimate and only Alpha - our Lord and Savior, Jesus Christ

INTRODUCTION

Instructions?

Yeah, I'm not a big fan of instructions either, but I want you to get the full benefit of this experience. It's simple - MAKE the time to read each day's prayer, scripture, and write out the Man Up and Pray Up sections.

You'll notice that there's plenty of space to write, draw, or do mathematical formulas. I don't like those either. But the point is, we are visual and hands-on. This life transformation book gives you room to roam.

Take advantage of it and do more than read this if you remember where you left it. Be active and change your life over the next 31 days. Oh, yeah and if you're reading this on an e-reader, don't try writing on the device; grab an old notebook or something.

Either you paid for this daily devotional, or someone who loves you bought it for you. Don't waste money or time! Make a commitment and work through this personal journal. I promise that the more you read, pray and write; the more you will benefit from it.

I have prayed over every day of this adventure and I know the words will speak to your soul because they aren't my words, they belong to God.

I'm also praying over you.

Much Love & Respect,
Scott

LET'S ROLL

Dear Warrior In Christ,

One of the most powerful moments in my life was when someone laid their hands on me in church, and I heard them begin to pray out loud for me.

The heat in my body rose, and I felt pure energy radiating through me. While both feet were bolted to the floor, my spirit soared at the words my brother spoke over me.

I believe in the power of prayer. I also believe in the God-ordained the powerful act of men praying for each other. Even as a Chief of Police, I would stop what I was doing to pray for brothers in need as the Lord moved me.

That's what this devotional is all about. Each day I asked God to move in me through the Holy Spirit to give me words for various areas in your life. Every day, God placed a very specific word on my heart that I wrote to be shared with you.

I'm not a professional pastor, nor do I speak eloquently, but when I pray, I know my words hold the power of our almighty God, and that His messages are meant for warriors like you.

Much Love & Respect,
Scott

DAY 1 PRAYER

Lord God,

Sin shackles us to hell. Confession is our key to freedom. Lord, show our brothers that the way to cleanse their burdens is through confession.

Teach our brothers confession is not weakness, but strength through submission to You. I pray our brothers lean upon Your promise in 1 John 1:9. I pray this day for men to become mighty men. Men who delight in Your presence, who treasure their wife, and commit completely to their children.

Show our brothers that redemption will never be found in work, no matter how hard they toil, but in the peace of surrender.

In the precious name of Jesus we pray, Amen.

GOD MADE MAN DAILY DEVOTION

> "If we confess our sins, He is faithful and just and will forgive us our sins and purify us from all unrighteousness."
>
> 1 John 1:9

MANLY ADVICE

"There is one rule, above all others, for being a man. Whatever comes, face it on your feet."

- Robert Jordan

MAN UP

This is your private prayer journal. Write the name of one person you hold a grudge against. You must forgive this person so that you will know freedom from their offense. Start with their name and write what you'd say to them.

PRAY UP

Write your own prayer for today. It may be for your wife, kids, or yourself. Whatever God lays on your heart, write it out as a prayer.

DAY 2 PRAYER

Lord God,

I pray for our brothers who have allowed other gods to come before You. Maybe it's sports, hunting, partying, their wife, or kids. Lord, show them that anything, no matter what it is or how helpful it might be, is to take a backseat to You.

If it's a god much worse than listed above, I ask that You show our brothers the way to healing. Lord, too many brothers are trapped by their lust in addictions, adultery, and sexual sin. Help them, Father, to see how destructive these obsessions are.

They not only steal the light away from You, but they bury men even farther into slavery.

Help our brothers understand that by focusing on You, that You shall care and provide for the rest. I thank You for Your words in Exodus 20:3 and Deuteronomy 5:7.

In the precious name of Jesus we pray, Amen.

GOD MADE MAN DAILY DEVOTION

Thou shalt have no other gods before me.

Exodus 20:3
&
Deuteronomy 5:7

MANLY ADVICE

> Can we continue to crawl through the same daily grind? Sure, and we might just reach the grand old age of average life expectancy. But wouldn't you rather steal home base with a scorching headfirst dive while avoiding an All-Star catcher?
>
> Dr. Scott Silverii
>
> From: *God Made Man: Discovering Your Purpose and Living an Intentional Life*

MAN UP

This is your private prayer journal. Write out the name of one person that you want forgiveness from. Then write out what you did to offend them, and a plea to Christ for forgiveness.

PRAY UP

Write your own prayer for today. It may be for your wife, kids, or yourself. Whatever God lays on your heart, write it out as a prayer.

DAY 3 PRAYER

Lord Father,

My heart breaks for brothers who suffer from feelings of loneliness. Our sisters are so much better at meeting and making true friendships, that we men are often left alone, feeling unloved.

I pray that our brothers drop the hard shell and make themselves approachable to other brothers so that the Holy Spirit can introduce them to each other. The darkness of loneliness can become suffocating, but still brothers cling to their pride.

Father, show them there are many others in the same circumstance praying to escape the crush of solitude. You did not make us to be alone. Whether it is a friend or a co-worker, men naturally seek bonding with other men. This is how early man survived—by creating tribes, villages and communities. Lord, I pray they know they are not alone.

In the precious name of Jesus we pray, Amen.

GOD MADE MAN DAILY DEVOTION

"And though one can overpower him who is alone, two can resist him. A cord of three strands is not quickly broken."

~ Ecclesiastes 4:12

MANLY ADVICE

> *There are two questions a man has to ask:*
>
> *The first is, 'Where am I going?' and the second is, 'Who will go with me?' If you ever get these questions in the wrong order you are in trouble."*
>
> \- Sam Keen

MAN UP

This is your private prayer journal. Write down the name of one person who was a positive force in your life. Then write out what you'd like to say to them.

PRAY UP

Write your own prayer for today. It may be for your wife, kids, or yourself. Whatever God lays on your heart, write it out as a prayer.

DAY 4 PRAYER

Lord God,

You've placed the word covetousness on my heart to share with our brothers. We lose sight of the many blessings You give because we're too busy drooling over what the neighbor has, or what some celebrity on TV is driving, or what an athlete is wearing.

I pray that they turn their eyes from others and lift their hearts to You. That they shall see how amazingly giving You are.

Blessings are often where we seek them. If a brother is reading this, then having the liberty of being free to worship is just one of many blessings You provide.

Covetousness also places the desired item above their love for You. I pray nothing interferes with their heavenly line of sight.

In the precious name of Jesus we pray, Amen.

GOD MADE MAN DAILY DEVOTION

> "You shall not covet your neighbor's house. You shall not covet your neighbor's wife, or his male or female servant, his ox or donkey, or anything that belongs to your neighbor."
>
> ~ Exodus 20:17

MANLY ADVICE

"And let's be honest, not every man is going to want to improve by drawing into a posture reflecting God. Some men are happy to wake up and see that there's not a police chalk line drawn around their body. They figure that they've lucked out another day, so why not get up, take their chances and see what happens while they're awake."

Dr. Scott Silverii

From: *God Made Man: Discovering Your Purpose and Living an Intentional Life*

MAN UP

This is your private prayer journal. This is going to hurt, but you've got to expose pain to light for healing. Write down the ten worst things that happened to you since your youth.

PRAY UP

Write your own prayer for today. It may be for your wife, kids, or yourself. Whatever God lays on your heart, write it out as a prayer.

DAY 5 PRAYER

Dear Lord,

I pray that You show our brothers how to deal with the anger that rages in their hearts. It is not a sin to be angry, but it is a sin to sin for the sake of anger. Anger is a human emotion that You blessed us with.

I pray that brothers do not allow it to control them, or to destroy them. If we have sinned against someone, please ask forgiveness. If someone has sinned against you and you are angry, forgive them.

Allow brothers to understand that forgiveness isn't about accepting the other's actions, it's about freeing themselves from the anger caused by the offense. Paul also reminds us in Ephesians that although we do get angry, that we are not to let the sun go down while still mad.

In the precious name of Jesus we pray, Amen.

GOD MADE MAN DAILY DEVOTION

> *"Be you angry, and sin not: let not the sun go down on your wrath"*
>
> ~ Ephesians 4:26

MANLY ADVICE

"*Men, you'll never be a good groom to your wife unless you're first a good bride to Jesus.*"

~ Timothy J. Keller

MAN UP

This is your private prayer journal. Write down the name of one friend who you wish you'd been a better friend to. Then write what it was that prevented you from being that better friend.

PRAY UP

Write your own prayer for today. It may be for your wife, kids, or yourself. Whatever God lays on your heart, write it out as a prayer.

DAY 6 PRAYER

Lord Father,

I pray for dads struggling over relationships with their children. You made parents to be Your image bearer. The young ones were meant to grow up to know You by watching and learning from their parents.

It seems so simple, but because man's separation from You through sin, this relationship is rarely simple. Our children's rejection is like a knife to our heart, and it covers dads with darkness. We dads carry so much guilt over strained and lost relationships that we often suffer the regrets for having condemned our kids to the potential cycle of generational sin we have experienced, because of strained relationships with our own dads.

Lord, I pray our brothers do not beat themselves up over the mistakes in parenting. I thank You for forgiving and restoring us so that we may continue to be present and active in their lives.

In the precious name of Jesus we pray, Amen.

GOD MADE MAN DAILY DEVOTION

"He will restore the hearts of the fathers to their children and the hearts of the children to their fathers, so that I will not come and smite the land with a curse."

~ Malachi 4:6

MANLY ADVICE

"Once we commit to dropping the tattered bags holding our busted trophies and dog-eared certificates, and seek God's purpose, then we'll understand His desire for our lives."

Dr. Scott Silverii

From: *God Made Man: Discovering Your Purpose and Living an Intentional Life*

MAN UP

This is your private prayer journal. This is the time for you to write out at least one more thing that you need to get off of your chest. Don't pull punches with God. It's time to dig deep and seek His will for your life.

PRAY UP

Write your own prayer for today. It may be for your wife, kids, or yourself. Whatever God lays on your heart, write it out as a prayer.

_____
_____
_____
_____
_____
_____
_____

DAY 7 PRAYER

Lord God,

I'm asking You for reconciliation for Brothers struggling in a marriage. You created marriage to reflect the intimate relationship we are to share with You. Your first miracle with man was the creation of woman and their union.

Jesus confirmed the value of marriage when His very first miracle was at a wedding. Revelations ends with the marriage supper. I pray for Brothers who are unsure or flat worn out over what to do to gain clarity to see the path You have set for them. Father, if they've sinned, please help them to understand the power of confession and the grace of forgiveness.

Lord, I know the devil hates marriage, and he's working overtime to rip them apart. I pray in the name of Jesus Christ for supernatural protection for our Brothers while they clear the path toward reconciling with their wives.

In the precious name of Jesus we pray, Amen.

GOD MADE MAN DAILY DEVOTION

Be kind to one another, tenderhearted, forgiving one another, as God in Christ forgave you.

~ Ephesians 4:32

MANLY ADVICE

"*A man should be able to hear, and to bear, the worst that could be said of him.*"

~ Saul Bellow

MAN UP

This is your private prayer journal. Write out your most favorite memory with your dad.

PRAY UP

Write your own prayer for today. It may be for your wife, kids, or yourself. Whatever God lays on your heart, write it out as a prayer.

DAY 8 PRAYER

Dear Father,

I pray for finances. So many brothers are worried or consumed by finances. It's halfway through the month and they're anxious about making it the rest of the way. Lord, this is Satan working to shake their foundation.

You want an abundant life for us and promised to meet our needs. I know this doesn't mean to make a shopping wish list, but You want our brothers to seek Your will for their life. You will provide for the desires placed in their hearts. Father, I pray that our brothers hold faithful and learn to increase by giving away.

This begins with tithing 10%. It's not about giving money to a church; it's about being obedient to Your word. You do more when we do less. I pray a special blessing of peace over our brothers. Grant them an opportunity to experience the joy of life without the worry of paying bills.

In the precious name of Jesus we pray, Amen.

GOD MADE MAN DAILY DEVOTION

> "Give, and it will be given to you. Good measure, pressed down, shaken together, running over, will be put into your lap. For with the measure you use it will be measured back to you."
>
> ~ Luke 6:38

MANLY ADVICE

"So how did we go from being God's right-hand man to getting kicked out and spawning generations of broken brothers? It was sin and its consequence of death. Of course, God made sure there was a better door to open before closing Adam's. In that second door is what the Bible refers to as the Second Adam. Not another failed natural-man, but a glorious victor in the spirit-man of Jesus Christ."

Dr. Scott Silverii

From: *God Made Man: Discovering Your Purpose and Living an Intentional Life*

MAN UP

This is your private prayer journal. Write out how you feel about your mom, and how the job she did raising you.

PRAY UP

Write your own prayer for today. It may be for your wife, kids, or yourself. Whatever God lays on your heart, write it out as a prayer.

DAY 9 PRAYER

Holy Father,

I pray for brothers struggling in their marriage or going through a divorce. You created the marriage covenant, and I pray they understand the significance of that eternal oath.

Genesis 2:25 "Therefore, a man shall leave his father and his mother and hold fast to his wife, and they shall become one flesh."

Father, You knew that it was not good for man to be alone (Genesis 2:18) so You created woman to be joined with man and even brought her to him (Genesis 2:22). In the first marriage ceremony in history, You said, *"a man shall leave his father and his mother and hold fast to his wife, and they shall become one flesh"* (Genesis 2:24).

This holy matrimony uses language that typifies what it means to become husband and wife. The two become "one flesh," meaning that they are so unified that they actually become one.

They become one in unity, one in essence (as in family), one in purpose, and one in mind. The meaning of joined is like that of a bonding agent—like glue. This "joining" is so strong that it is like one part of the other will be ripped away from the other if they are ever separated.

If you joined two pieces of paper with glue and tore them apart, each sheet of paper would take with it part of the other. This is a great image of what divorce does. It damages both parties so much that both are hurt in the process, therefore they should cleave and not leave, because what You have joined together, no one should try to separate.

In the precious name of Jesus we pray, Amen.

GOD MADE MAN DAILY DEVOTION

> *"Therefore, a man shall leave his father and his mother and hold fast to his wife, and they shall become one flesh."*
>
> ~ Genesis 2:25

MANLY ADVICE

A man's ledger does not tell what he is, or what he is worth. Count what is in man, not what is on him, if you would know what he is worth— whether rich or poor.

~ Henry Ward Beecher

MAN UP

This is your private prayer journal. Write out three things you wish you hadn't done in the last 10 years and what were their consequences.

PRAY UP

Write your own prayer for today. It may be for your wife, kids, or yourself. Whatever God lays on your heart, write it out as a prayer.

DAY 10 PRAYER

Holy Father,

Today You have placed the burden of infidelity on my heart. Lord, I pray for our brothers who battle the flesh. Father, I said the burden of infidelity instead of saying the sin of infidelity because our brothers understand it is a grave sin, but most do not understand that it is a burden.

Many brothers who act out sexually do not know why they do so. Many promise to behave and be loyal, and in their hearts, they truly do wish to be faithful. But the chains of Satan's temptation to pursue the flesh is more powerful than our brothers' will to flee.

This, my Lord is their burden, which causes their sin. Brothers continue to relive this act of defiance, oath-breaking, and covetousness each time they flirt, text, bait-click pornography, steal a simple kiss at the after work happy-hour, or commit to long-term or repeated sexual affairs.

I pray that they seek Your will to delete, erase, or block women who they hide from their wife on social media or texting. Help them know the joy of marital purity by busting those chains that drag them down through sexual sin.

In the precious name of Jesus we pray, Amen.

GOD MADE MAN DAILY DEVOTION

> *Flee from sexual immorality. Every other sin a person commits is outside the body, but the sexually immoral person sins against his own body.*
>
> ~ 1 Corinthians 6:18

MANLY ADVICE

> "Prosperity comes in many forms but those such as your relationship to God, your spouse, family, health, peace, love and joy are so much more vital than cash in your pocket."
>
> ~ Dr. Scott Silverii
>
> From: *God Made Man: Discovering Your Purpose and Living an Intentional Life*

MAN UP

This is your private prayer journal. Write out the name of one person who caused you grief as a child. Then explain how that makes you feel still today.

PRAY UP

Write your own prayer for today. It may be for your wife, kids, or yourself. Whatever God lays on your heart, write it out as a prayer.

DAY 11 PRAYER

Dear Father,

I pray for brothers who have hurt someone they loved and are now struggling with not asking for forgiveness. I also pray that they gain a clear understanding of what forgiveness means. Too often people refuse to forgive others.

God, You are very clear that if we do not forgive others, that You will not forgive us. I pray that our brothers humble themselves before those they have wronged by asking them to forgive them. Please show our brothers that being forgiven also does not mean the hurtful action has been forgotten.

Many times brothers ask for prayer that their spouse returns and that they have changed. Too often these brothers expect their wife to forgive and forget what they did to hurt them. While they may forgive, it may require time and patience for the trust to return. This, my Lord, is where many brothers get impatient and turn against their wives because she may still be struggling with the offense that first hurt them.

Father, I pray that our brothers learn to say, "I'm sorry," and "Please forgive me." When they cause pain through their actions. I pray that they truly repent and see the wrong that they do and the damage that they cause.

I pray that You soften the hardness of their hearts and allow them to know what being forgiven really feels like. It was You that forgave us of our sins, and You that allowed Your Son to die because of our sins. We praise You for the gift of grace and salvation.

In the precious name of Jesus we pray, Amen.

GOD MADE MAN DAILY DEVOTION

> *Therefore, confess your sins to one another and pray for one another, that you may be healed. The prayer of a righteous person has great power as it is working.*
>
> ~ James 5:16

MANLY ADVICE

> "We do not admire the man of timid peace. We admire the man who embodies victorious effort; the man who never wrongs his neighbor, who is prompt to help a friend, but who has those virile qualities necessary to win in the stern strife of actual life."
>
> ~ Theodore Roosevelt

MAN UP

This is your private prayer journal. Write out two regrets in your life. Then explain how they affected your life at the time, and now.

PRAY UP

Write your own prayer for today. It may be for your wife, kids, or yourself. Whatever God lays on your heart, write it out as a prayer.

DAY 12 PRAYER

Holy Lord,

I pray for mercy received and mercy shown. You placed the message of mercy on my heart to be shared with our brothers. Mercy is when we deserve to be punished because of our sin, but instead, we are spared the punishment by You, Lord.

I pray our brothers understand how often Your judgment is deserved because of our actions, but by Your mercy, we are spared. Father, with this in mind, I pray that our brothers also show mercy to those within their power to punish or discipline.

It's easy to withhold something of value or swing a hand to harm another, but it is by

Your example of sparing us when we deserve destruction, that I pray our brothers abide. True strength comes from showing mercy and mentoring the offending person toward the right path. Any bully can strike, but a true Christian brother will show mercy.

In the precious name of Jesus we pray, Amen.

GOD MADE MAN DAILY DEVOTION

So speak and so act as those who are to be judged under the law of liberty. For judgment is without mercy to one who has shown no mercy. Mercy triumphs over judgment.

~ James 2:12-13

MANLY ADVICE

"The truth is that God did not need us. He doesn't have an ego to pump or people to high-five. When you look back over the course of human history, we've pretty much made a mess of things. So, when the Bible says to glorify Him, it is only out of His love that we were created, and for love that we remain. We were created out of God, so in us is a piece of Him. Because He is love, then we too are a reflection of that love."

Dr. Scott Silverii

From: *God Made Man: Discovering Your Purpose and Living an Intentional Life*

MAN UP

This is your private prayer journal. This is the time for you to write out another thing that you need to get off of your chest. Don't pull punches with God, it's time to dig deep and seek His will for your life.

PRAY UP

Write your own prayer for today. It may be for your wife, kids, or yourself. Whatever God lays on your heart, write it out as a prayer.

DAY 13 PRAYER

Dear Father,

As I sit across from my wife, I'm moved to pray for Godly women. I pray our brothers understand the eternal value of having a woman in their life who loves You first, Lord.

Father, I pray for women who seek Your heart with all of theirs. Church pews are filled with these virtuous women, yet too often they go unnoticed and unappreciated by the very men they are praying for. Father, I pray for these women.

I ask You to bless them for their faithfulness. Lord please allow them to always know they are loved, respected and protected by our brothers. Allow them to see Your face in the midst of their burdens for family. Show these blessed women that they truly are as Solomon said in Proverbs far above rubies.

In the precious name of Jesus we pray, Amen.

GOD MADE MAN DAILY DEVOTION

"Who can find a virtuous woman? For her price is far above rubies."

~ Proverbs 31:10

MANLY ADVICE

> "Relieved of moral pretense and stripped of folk costumes, the raw masculinity that all men know in their gut has to do with being good at being a man within a small, embattled gang of men struggling to survive."
>
> ~ Jack Donovan

MAN UP

This is your private prayer journal. Write out how your last significant relationship ended and why. Also, what would you have done better.

PRAY UP

Write your own prayer for today. It may be for your wife, kids, or yourself. Whatever God lays on your heart, write it out as a prayer.

DAY 14 PRAYER

Dear Lord,

I pray our brothers know how blessed and loved they are. No matter what obstacle are in their paths, or the worries that occupy their mind, I ask You to open their eyes and ears to know they are covered by the blood of Your Son, Jesus Christ.

No matter how bad they screwed up in life, that they do not get to control the story that You have written for them. I pray they come to know You, and trust that You have a plan for them. That they realize their life was not an accident, Each day shouldn't be lived only because they happened to wake up.

Our brothers are prayed for every day by us and they should see the Godly women who also lift them up. God, I beg that our brothers see they are no failure. That they can turn their stories around by turning them over to You. I pray our brothers feel the love and respect we give them in daily prayers. Let us pray without ceasing for our brothers to be the real, old-school men of men.

In the precious name of Jesus we pray, Amen.

GOD MADE MAN DAILY DEVOTION

"*Rejoice always, pray without ceasing, in everything give thanks; for this is the will of God in Christ Jesus for you.*"

~ 1 Thessalonians 5:16-18

MANLY ADVICE

"Don't let religion get in the way. It's unfortunate that once we feel the tug for Christ we get discouraged by rules and rituals of whatever church we happen to walk into. Don't confuse faith with religion. Too many religions turn people away from God because their focus is on what else? Joining their religion."

Dr. Scott Silverii

From: *God Made Man: Discovering Your Purpose and Living an Intentional Life*

MAN UP

This is your private prayer journal. Write about the first time you realized there was a God, and how your relationship with Him has progressed.

PRAY UP

Write your own prayer for today. It may be for your wife, kids, or yourself. Whatever God lays on your heart, write it out as a prayer.

DAY 15 PRAYER

Dear Lord,

I pray that we look at each other as our brother's keeper. I know the line is attributed to Cain when he killed Abel, but there are many references in Your word to one brother looking out after the other. I love Matthew 25:35...

"For I was hungry and you gave me food, I was thirsty and you gave me drink, I was a stranger and you welcomed me"

Father, I know following you isn't for wimps. You called us to be men and to expect tough times because we love You. You said we will be persecuted for Your name's sake, but that we would be blessed.

Dear Father, I pray a blessing for these brothers because they have taken a stand for You, and they have stood among one another as their brother's friend and keeper.

In the precious name of Jesus we pray, Amen.

GOD MADE MAN DAILY DEVOTION

"Blessed are you when people insult you and persecute you, and falsely say all kinds of evil against you because of Me.

~ Matthew 5:11

MANLY ADVICE

"We don't need to reinvent manliness. We only need to will ourselves to wake up from the bad dream of the last few generations and reclaim it, in order to extend and enrich that tradition under the formidable demands of the present."

~ Waller R. Newell

MAN UP

This is your private prayer journal. Write out about how you feel you handle money and finances. Are you financially secure? If not, what do you need to change in your behavior?

PRAY UP

Write your own prayer for today. It may be for your wife, kids, or yourself. Whatever God lays on your heart, write it out as a prayer.

DAY 16 PRAYER

Dear Lord,

I am so thankful for my wife and our marriage. She and our marriage are gifts, and I value it because I love the Gift Giver – You. You know I've not always acted to show my love, and I thank You for Your grace.

Our marriage endures because of our covenant with You. Father, I pray for our married brothers to see the significance of their own covenants between their wives and You. Father, show our brothers the power of a covenant, and that it is not a simple "contract" that can be broken.

Lord, show our brothers that while a contract generally has a term limit, covenants are eternal. Contracts are designed as a way for both parties to "get" something, covenants are filled by Your grace. Contracts deal with an "if...then" mentality.

The first step to divorce-proofing their marriage is to stop thinking of their union as an "if...then," and start thinking in terms of eternity.

In the precious name of Jesus we pray, Amen.

GOD MADE MAN DAILY DEVOTION

> *However, let each one of you love his wife as himself, and let the wife see that she respects her husband.*
>
> ~ Ephesians 5:33

MANLY ADVICE

"So now that you've asked Christ into your life, it's time to learn more about Him. It's like accepting a roommate into your condo. Y'all are going to be living together and hanging out, so wouldn't you want to know everything about Him? Christ is that way, and the more you get to know Him, the more you'll want to be just like Him."

Dr. Scott Silverii

From: *God Made Man: Discovering Your Purpose and Living an Intentional Life*

MAN UP

This is your private prayer journal. Write out the name of one person who made you feel small or like you didn't matter. Then write how that makes you feel now.

PRAY UP

Write your own prayer for today. It may be for your wife, kids, or yourself. Whatever God lays on your heart, write it out as a prayer.

_____

_____

_____

_____

_____

_____

_____

DAY 17 PRAYER

Dear Father,
I pray for our brothers who suffer from the three I's. Brother like to deal in areas of being respected, and capable, but to suddenly find ourselves Invisible, Irrelevant or Isolated terrifies us.

Father, this usually happens because our shame or hurt causes us to avoid other people. Even family and friends. Lord, this also causes our brothers to avoid You. Men speak and respond to terms of respect, so I pray our brothers will know they are respected when they stand for You.

They may fear being outcasts among their current friends, but eternally, these aren't the friends our brothers need in their lives right now. Lord, I pray for strength and boldness for our brothers who are suffering from one or all three of the I's - Invisible, Irrelevant or Isolated. I pray they turn to You to be Seen, Substantial and Surrounded.

In the precious name of Jesus we pray, Amen.

GOD MADE MAN DAILY DEVOTION

Benaiah son of Jehoiada, a valiant fighter from Kabzeel, performed great exploits. He struck down Moab's two mightiest warriors. He also went down into a pit on a snowy day and killed a lion. And he struck down a huge Egyptian. Although the Egyptian had a spear in his hand, Benaiah went against him with a club. He snatched the spear from the Egyptian's hand and killed him with his own spear.

~ 2 Samuel 23:20-21

MANLY ADVICE

> *"If unwilling to rise in the morning, say to thyself, 'I awake to do the work of a man.'"*
>
> ~ Marcus Aurelius

MAN UP

This is your private prayer journal. Are you in the job you want? If so, how did you accomplish that? If not, write out why not.

PRAY UP

Write your own prayer for today. It may be for your wife, kids, or yourself. Whatever God lays on your heart, write it out as a prayer.

DAY 18 PRAYER

Dear Father,

I pray for a word. Lord, I pray You whisper a word to our brothers who want to follow You, and also brothers who are believers, but have not heard Your voice in a long time. Let them know You are there.

Men are visual and need proof before making big decisions. The disciple, Thomas asked You for evidence, and You were gracious to show him where you were pierced. It didn't make Thomas a bad guy for doubting, it just showed his natural suspicion.

He was in a tough time, just as we are living in tough times. There is so much misinformation about everything that we often don't know where to turn. Who can we trust after all? It's simple—we can trust You.

Please help our brothers get over the hump of not trusting or knowing what to believe. Place Your word in their heart and allow them to know they were once again touched by Your grace.

In the precious name of Jesus we pray, Amen.

GOD MADE MAN DAILY DEVOTION

> *"Show me what you want me to do. You are my God. Let your good Spirit lead me over level ground."*
>
> ~ Psalms 143:10

MANLY ADVICE

"Pursuing God's will is what begins separating us from the past of pain, failure and sin that once defined us. We don't have the capacity in our natural-man to just stop patterns that have become engrained throughout our life. Change comes first from the spirit-man because as God promises, we are new creations in Christ."

Dr. Scott Silverii
From: *God Made Man: Discovering Your Purpose and Living an Intentional Life*

MAN UP

This is your private prayer journal. This is the time for you to write out at least one thing that you need to get off of your chest. Don't pull punches with God, it's time to dig deep and seek His will for your life.

PRAY UP

Write your own prayer for today. It may be for your wife, kids, or yourself. Whatever God lays on your heart, write it out as a prayer.

DAY 19 PRAYER

Dear God,

I pray for our brothers seeking marital purity, but who are stuck with the black mark of unconfessed adultery. One in four husbands cheat on the woman they swore before You to love, honor, and cherish.

Father, there are many reasons why our brothers wander away from the gift You gave them but help them to know that no excuses are acceptable in Your eyes. Help them to see also that their actions are forgivable sins, but that they must trust You to confess in sincerity and reform.

Only You can change the desires of a willing heart. I pray for this generation of men to stand beside their wife and resist the temptations.

In the precious name of Jesus we pray, Amen.

GOD MADE MAN DAILY DEVOTION

"To preserve you from the evil woman, from the smooth tongue of the adulteress. Do not desire her beauty in your heart, and do not let her capture you with her eyelashes; for the price of a prostitute is only a loaf of bread, but a married woman hunts down a precious life. Can a man carry fire next to his chest and his clothes not be burned? Or can one walk on hot coals and his feet not be scorched?..."

~ Proverbs 6:24-29

MANLY ADVICE

> *"A man's got to have a code, a creed to live by, no matter his job."*
>
> ~ John Wayne

MAN UP

This is your private prayer journal. Write out the name of the last person you felt hatred for. What made so furious, and how did you get over it? You did, didn't you?

```
_____
_____
_____
_____
_____
_____
```

PRAY UP

Write your own prayer for today. It may be for your wife, kids, or yourself. Whatever God lays on your heart, write it out as a prayer.

DAY 20 PRAYER

Dear Father,

I pray for our brothers living beneath the dark cloud of shame. We men encounter so much throughout each day that it's easy to do something, whether intentional or not, that brings us into a sin relationship.

This, of course, separates us from You. Shame is another destructive weapon launched by the devil to tarnish the shine of manhood. Please help our brothers to hold themselves and each other accountable through prayer and confession.

Allow this to help lift the burden of shame we carry. Lift up our brothers and allow them to experience the joy and power of pursuing purity and Your will for their lives. There really is power in the blood.

In the precious name of Jesus we pray, Amen.

GOD MADE MAN DAILY DEVOTION

But the Lord God helps me; therefore I have not been disgraced; therefore I have set my face like a flint, and I know that I shall not be put to shame.

~ Isaiah 50:7

MANLY ADVICE

"What is your identity attached to? Has God tugged on certain areas of your life, but you tugged back? Are you more focused on being The Man than on being God's son? Let's take a peek at exactly what it looks like to be God's son, and the man He called to serve His kingdom by following Him and leading your household. It may look a lot different from how you imagined."

Dr. Scott Silverii
From: *God Made Man: Discovering Your Purpose and Living an Intentional Life*

MAN UP

This is your private prayer journal. Write out what you are most afraid of. Explain where that fear came from and what, if anything, have you done to overcome it.

PRAY UP

Write your own prayer for today. It may be for your wife, kids, or yourself. Whatever God lays on your heart, write it out as a prayer.

DAY 21 PRAYER

Lord Father,

Hallelujah that You are the Great Healer. Lord, we as men suffer in silence. We've mistakenly accepted this as a sign of strength, when in fact it's a darkness in our spirits that prevents overcoming past and present hurts.

Father, help our brothers examine their lives and identify past pains that now cause current hurts, anger, or bad actions against themselves or others. Show them that the only way to heal that pain is to bring light to it.

You, Father are that light. Show our brothers to call out to You and confess sins and pray for healing from their wounds. You are the Healer and Redeemer!!

In the precious name of Jesus we pray, Amen.

GOD MADE MAN DAILY DEVOTION

Fear not, for I am with you; be not dismayed, for I am your God; I will strengthen you, I will help you, I will uphold you with my righteous right hand.

~ Isaiah 41:10

MANLY ADVICE

There is nothing noble being superior to your fellow man; true nobility is being superior to your former self.

~ Winston Churchill

MAN UP

This is your private prayer journal. Yep, you guessed it. Its time again for you to write out at least one thing that you need to get off of your chest. Don't pull punches with God, it's time to dig deep and seek His will for your life.

PRAY UP

Write your own prayer for today. It may be for your wife, kids, or yourself. Whatever God lays on your heart, write it out as a prayer.

DAY 22 PRAYER

Dear Father,

I pray for brothers struggling with one or more of the 3 A's. Too often, we fail at Adultery, Addiction, or Anger. I pray for our brothers who are seeking a way out of the devil's tactics.

So often, any of these A's are rooted in pain from our brothers' pasts. So often, our childhood or parents left wounds on our souls that have never healed. These injuries can lead to adultery, addiction, and anger.

Father, show these brothers it is okay to open up and seek healing. Getting better is not a sign of weakness. It is a great strength.

Please show them the hurt they cause others because they hurt inside too. This isn't a prayer for the weak, my Lord.

This is a plea for strong, respectable men to feel the value of self-worth and being healed from their past, so they will stop hurting the ones they love with the 3 A's.

In the precious name of Jesus we pray, Amen.

GOD MADE MAN DAILY DEVOTION

He will wipe away every tear from their eyes, and death shall be no more, neither shall there be mourning, nor crying, nor pain anymore, for the former things have passed away."

~ Revelation 21:4

MANLY ADVICE

"There is a process of pursuing God's forgiveness throughout our trials and stumbles. When we fall, God is there to give us a hand up, but we've still got to be willing to reach out."

Dr. Scott Silverii

From: *God Made Man: Discovering Your Purpose and Living an Intentional Life*

MAN UP

This is your private prayer journal. If you are married , write a prayer for your wife. If not, pray for someone significant in your life.

PRAY UP

Write your own prayer for today. It may be for your wife, kids, or yourself. Whatever God lays on your heart, write it out as a prayer.

DAY 23 PRAYER

Lord,

I pray for our brothers who are blessed to be married. I ask that You inspire them to pursue marital purity. You created marriage to reflect our relationship with You.

Because You are the gift giver, the way we treat our wife reflects not only on us men, but on how we love You. Father, marital purity is not a subject often discussed among men.

The crude locker room chatter still prevails in and outside of the room. I pray our brothers open their hearts to the destruction of those words and consider speaking of their wife and any woman with respect.

Lord, I pray that if anyone is considering infidelity that they would flee from temptation. Show them that's it's not the coward who runs, but the dead who tempt the powerful enemy of sexual sin.

In the precious name of Jesus we pray, Amen.

GOD MADE MAN DAILY DEVOTION

> *No temptation has overtaken you that is not common to man. God is faithful, and he will not let you be tempted beyond your ability, but with the temptation he will also provide the way of escape, that you may be able to endure it.*
>
> *~ 1 Corinthians 10:13*

MANLY ADVICE

It takes a great man to be a good listener.

~ Calvin Coolidge

MAN UP

This is your private prayer journal. How has your attitude about doing these 31 days of prayers changed from the first day you began your challenge?

PRAY UP

Write your own prayer for today. It may be for your wife, kids, or yourself. Whatever God lays on your heart, write it out as a prayer.

DAY 24 PRAYER

Dear Lord,

Praise You for family. Thank You for our parents and siblings. Father, we know not every family unit is supportive, caring or intact, but that doesn't prohibit the need to honor our mother and father.

Your word says nothing about judging our earthly parents, but that we are to honor them. I pray that if there is pain associated with a brother's family, that the model of honoring despite the injuries will allow them to follow Your example as being a Godly father to their kids so that the cycle of family dysfunction and strife ends at their generation.

Father, You are a good, good Father. We men can do better through You. I pray that Your heart for family will shine through to brothers still in the struggle to be the head of their household.

In the precious name of Jesus we pray, Amen.

GOD MADE MAN DAILY DEVOTION

But I want you to understand that the head of every man is Christ, the head of a wife is her husband, and the head of Christ is God.

~ 1 Corinthians 11:3

MANLY ADVICE

> "Being humble is a spiritual gift for some, while it takes getting the snot beat out of life to humble others. Either way, men cannot come into a Christlike posture without a very healthy dose of being humble."
>
> Dr. Scott Silverii
>
> From: *God Made Man: Discovering Your Purpose and Living an Intentional Life*

MAN UP

This is your private prayer journal. If God came back at this very moment, where would you go? Explain why you feel that way.

PRAY UP

Write your own prayer for today. It may be for your wife, kids, or yourself. Whatever God lays on your heart, write it out as a prayer.

DAY 25 PRAYER

Holy Father,

I pray that You show our brothers fighting the pull of pornography that there is a way out of their sexual bondage. Let them sincerely understand the damage they do to themselves and those around them by succumbing to the temptation of sexual sin.

Father, the secrets, the lies, and the deception associated with sexual sin are the chains used by the devil to lock men down into the bowels of hell. Men cannot overcome Satan without Your mighty authority.

Help them to seek the resources to lead them into a life changing decision to break those shackles. I pray, Father, that they will seek other brothers to hold them accountable and that they are not stopped by shame or guilt, but that they seek freedom through faith and confession.

In the precious name of Jesus we pray, Amen.

GOD MADE MAN DAILY DEVOTION

But I say, walk by the Spirit, and you will not gratify the desires of the flesh.

~ Galatians 5:16

MANLY ADVICE

A man does what he must -- in spite of personal consequences, in spite of obstacles and dangers, and pressures -- and that is the basis of all human morality.

~ John Kennedy

MAN UP

This is your private prayer journal. Do you need to forgive your dad? If so, what has he done or not done in your life that hurt you? What would you say to him?

PRAY UP

Write your own prayer for today. It may be for your wife, kids, or yourself. Whatever God lays on your heart, write it out as a prayer.

DAY 26 PRAYER

Lord God,

I pray that Your merciful hand lay down upon our brothers who are struggling to labor. Brothers who are out of work or who have lost the joy in the work they do.

Work is fulfilling for a man, and You bless the fruitful with more abundance than their efforts may produce. Lord, I ask Your grace for our brothers fighting to provide for their family, even if there doesn't seem to be a way.

Show them the path. Our brothers equate work with providing and being able to provide with respect. This causes so much stress and worry for men. It chips away at their true joy. I pray they may know peace in their labor and take the time to relax while with their family.

In the precious name of Jesus we pray, Amen.

GOD MADE MAN DAILY DEVOTION

> *Whatever you do, work heartily, as for the Lord and not for men, knowing that from the Lord you will receive the inheritance as your reward. You are serving the Lord Christ.*
>
> *~ Colossians 3:23-24*

MANLY ADVICE

"Being a servant is having a willing heart to do for others above yourself. Don't worry if this doesn't come natural to you. As you pursue Christ and really make an effort to connect with Him, the Holy Spirit enters into the picture as Jesus' helper to develop your spirit-man over the worldly habits of your natural-man."

Dr. Scott Silverii

From: *God Made Man: Discovering Your Purpose and Living an Intentional Life*

MAN UP

This is your private prayer journal. Write out three things that starting today, you can become better about. Then explain how you will go about being better.

PRAY UP

Write your own prayer for today. It may be for your wife, kids, or yourself. Whatever God lays on your heart, write it out as a prayer.

DAY 27 PRAYER

Lord God,

Place Your hand upon your army of men. Help us to heal from the pain of past hurts. We think by building a hard shell around our emotional man, that we are protected from attacks and injuries.

While the natural man may learn to endure the storms, it is the spirit man that withers within these walls. Not showing emotional vulnerability or allowing anyone to get close is a sure path to destruction and regret.

Show us that the hard shell we construct doesn't protect us from injury, it actually helps seal the hurts inside. Lord, help us to break the bricks that prevent us from healing.

In the precious name of Jesus we pray, Amen.

GOD MADE MAN DAILY DEVOTION

> *But he gives more grace. Therefore it says, "God opposes the proud, but gives grace to the humble."*
>
> ~ James 4:6

MANLY ADVICE

Men are like steel. When they lose their temper, they lose their worth.

~ Chuck Norris

MAN UP

This is your private prayer journal. Write out how you would feel if someone stole something from you. What would you do to get it back and what would you do to that person?

PRAY UP

Write your own prayer for today. It may be for your wife, kids, or yourself. Whatever God lays on your heart, write it out as a prayer.

DAY 28 PRAYER

Dear Father,

I pray that You show our brothers the power of prayer. I ask that they read Your word in 1 John 5:14-15 and have the boldness to ask and the confidence to expect their prayers to become one with Your will.

Lord, show our brothers how to pray with expectancy, but also show them first how to clear the path of sin debris that blocks the direct communication with you. Too many believers toil in vain over prayers that will not be answered.

Not because You don't love them, but because unconfessed sin and unrepentant hearts interfere with the intimacy You seek.

I pray they come into a close and constant conversation with their loving Father, who is so willing to answer their petitions.

In the precious name of Jesus we pray, Amen.

GOD MADE MAN DAILY DEVOTION

"And this is the confidence that we have toward him, that if we ask anything according to his will he hears us. And if we know that he hears us in whatever we ask, we know that we have the requests that we have asked of him."

~ 1 John 5:14-15

MANLY ADVICE

I'm not sure who started the rumor that believers can only practice the missionary position, but while it's a good move, there are no restrictions on the expression of love between husband and wife. While there are boundaries, they are meant as guidelines to protect what is valuable in your marriage and sexual relationship:

- Sex is only between you and your wife. No other people, porn or mental fantasies of others.
- Is it mutually pleasurable for the both of you?
- Anything goes as long as both of you consent to it.

Dr. Scott Silverii

From: *God Made Man: Discovering Your Purpose and Living an Intentional Life*

MAN UP

This is your private prayer journal. Are you the biblical man of the house? If so, explain why you feel that way. If not, what will you do to improve?

PRAY UP

Write your own prayer for today. It may be for your wife, kids, or yourself. Whatever God lays on your heart, write it out as a prayer.

DAY 29 PRAYER

Dear Lord,

Help our brothers to remain all in with their family. Encourage brothers to engage with their wife and kids when they are together. To be the man that You created them to be.

Holy, righteous, bold and loving. Our families need us to lead the team. Switch off the TV or internet and allow those who love you and look up to you and get to know you.

Putting your phone down will open up incredible streams of communications with family and other believers. Father, you ordained men to be the mirror of You.

You made us so perfectly in Your image so our kids can learn about You through their mom and dads. Lord the only way for others to see the Christ in them is to go all in with their time, attention, love and focus on the family.

In the precious name of Jesus we pray, Amen.

GOD MADE MAN DAILY DEVOTION

Then God said, "Let Us make man in Our image, according to Our likeness; and let them rule over the fish of the sea and over the birds of the sky and over the cattle and over all the earth, and over every creeping thing that creeps on the earth." So God created mankind in his own image, in the image of God he created them; male and female he created them.

~ Genesis 1:26-27

MANLY ADVICE

It is not titles that make men illustrious, but men who make titles illustrious.

~ Machiavelli

MAN UP

This is your private prayer journal. Write you what you understand a God-centered life looks like.

PRAY UP

Write your own prayer for today. It may be for your wife, kids, or yourself. Whatever God lays on your heart, write it out as a prayer.

DAY 30 PRAYER

Lord God,

I pray for peace for my brothers. You know their struggles. They may be with finances, addiction, adultery, depression, or self-doubt. You know they are NOT broken but wounded.

Help them to commit their troubles to You and leave them at the foot of the cross for You to address. Father, so often we men avoid looking back out of fear of what we might see. The past is never as far away as we would like to think.

It's within that past that so much pain was caused and created. Men prefer to forge ahead, when in reality instead of leaving our troubles behind, we are just dragging them along.

God, grant our brothers the courage to see what has really caused them pain, whether it was in their past or right in their face, allow them to seek Your healing.

In the precious name of Jesus we pray, Amen.

GOD MADE MAN DAILY DEVOTION

> *"You shall not worship them or serve them; for I, the LORD your God, am a jealous God, visiting the iniquity of the fathers on the children, on the third and the fourth generations of those who hate Me."*
>
> ~ Exodus 20:5

MANLY ADVICE

"It's only when our will is in alignment with God that we rise above subjecting ourselves to instantaneous personal whims and temporary physical desires. I'm sure I don't have to connect these dots to what we call sin. Anything outside of what God intimately desires for us leads to sin. It's not a control power trip, but it is that all He wants is what is good and best for us."

Dr. Scott Silverii

From: *God Made Man: Discovering Your Purpose and Living an Intentional Life*

MAN UP

This is your private prayer journal. What makes you feel unworthy or unwanted? Explain how those factors influence you in that way, and what will you do to change.

PRAY UP

Write your own prayer for today. It may be for your wife, kids, or yourself. Whatever God lays on your heart, write it out as a prayer.

DAY 31 PRAYER

Dear Father,

Hallelujah for these last 31 days. You have spoken life, love respect and healing our men. They are so precious to You and respected within the kingdom.

Father, these last generations have attacked men for being men. Their power and masculinity has been insulted with efforts by the devil to corrode and water down what Your word describes as manhood.

I am so thankful that You allowed this prayer book to become reality and pray it has been a blessing. I pray that each section has been filled out by a beloved brother. If they didn't have time to search their soul during the prayers,

I ask they take the time very soon and write, think, or pray through their relationship with You.

God, I pray this brother comes to know You in a deeper way than they've ever imagined.

In the precious name of Jesus we pray, Amen.

GOD MADE MAN DAILY DEVOTION

"For the Lord God is a sun and shield; the Lord bestows favor and honor; no good thing does He withhold from those who walk uprightly."

~ Psalm 84:11

MANLY ADVICE

Big jobs usually go to the men who prove their ability to outgrow small ones.

~ Theodore Roosevelt

MAN UP

This is your private prayer journal. Write out your personal testimony. And then pat yourself on the back for rocking out a 31-day prayer challenge. Great going!

PRAY UP

Write your own prayer for today. It may be for your wife, kids, or yourself. Whatever God lays on your heart, write it out as a prayer.

PREVIEW - GOD MADE MAN

"I'm leaving."

It was the final straw in what had been a horrible year since I retired as a chief of police in another state and relocated to Dallas with my family.

Slamming the door behind me, I marched into the cold, driving rain. Juggling the keys in my palm, I still wasn't sure where it was, I was going, or why. But I'd had enough.

Retirement was supposed to be an incredible, carefree adventure. Leah and I would do all of the things we wanted to do and go places we wanted to see. Easy life, right?

I slipped as I ran through the rain to get into my Jeep. I also failed to avoid the smash of rainwater that dashed over the lip of the canvas top and dumped across my shirt's sleeve. I didn't care anymore. I just wanted out.

Soon, I became twisted in the madness of what is known as Dallas traffic. I desperately peered through sheets of water washing over my windshield, and finally threw the phone to the floorboard because I couldn't get service to strike up the GPS. I thought I knew where the medical clinic was located, so if I could only get within striking distance, I could figure out the rest. Sure, Leah and I had argued about me going there, but after a year of stress, deep depression, weight gain and loneliness, I was desperate for help and wasn't sure where else to look.

For some crazy reason, I was trying to find a weight loss clinic. I'd ballooned up to 270 pounds, my blood pressure was rocketing so high my eyes actually throbbed, and all I wanted to do was sleep. Shoving me deeper into darkness was the reality that only a year prior, I had been "The Man" back in my south Louisiana city. I was a well-known chief of police, a college professor and an expert national speaker on everything from data-driven policing to mystery writing.

As I frantically watched for street signs and avoiding rear bumpers, I was lost in a city where no one knew my name, offered no free passes because I once wore a badge, or recognized me as "Chief." It wasn't until two hours later that I skulked back home. Truthfully, I was so lost that I'd never traveled more than four miles from where I'd started. I was lost, alone, and worst of all; I was no longer The Man.

Standing in the driving rain outside of our home's darkened front door, I tugged my sopping wet shirt over the paddle holster in my waistband. My elbow tapped against the pistol's grip out of weapon retention habit. It would've been so easy to be done with it right then and there. The kids weren't home, and Leah knew I'd been struggling over a final solution. I hesitated because I knew there were only two choices left for me in this life. Let me tell you about the one I chose.

DR. SCOTT SILVERII

Dr. Scott Silverii is a son of the Living God. Thankful for the gift of his wife, Leah, they share seven kids, a French bulldog named Bacon and a micro-mini Goldendoodle named Biscuit.

A highly decorated, twenty-five-year law enforcement career promptly ended in retirement when God called Scott out of public service and into HIS service. The "Chief" admits that leading people to Christ is more exciting than the twelve years he spent undercover, sixteen years in SWAT, and five years as chief of police combined.

Scott has earned post-doctoral hours in a Doctor of Ministry degree in addition to a Master of Public Administration and a Ph.D. in Cultural Anthropology. Education and experience allow for a deeper understanding in ministering to the wounded, as he worked to break free from his own past pain and abuse.

In 2016, Scott was led to plant a church. Exclusive to online ministry, Five Stones Church.Online was born out of the calling to combat the negative influences reigning over social media. Scott's alpha manhood model for heroes is defined by, "Be on your guard; stand firm in the faith; be courageous; be strong. Do everything in love." (1 Corinthians 16:13-14)

www.ingramcontent.com/pod-product-compliance
Lightning Source LLC
Chambersburg PA
CBHW071959110526
44592CB00012B/1142